50 Chopsticks & Cheeseburgers Recipes

By: Kelly Johnson

Table of Contents

- Bulgogi Cheeseburger
- Kimchi Quesadilla
- Teriyaki Mac and Cheese
- Gochujang Chicken Tacos
- Korean Corn Dog Bites
- Miso Butter Ramen
- Sesame Sriracha Sliders
- Scallion Pancake Wraps
- Pork Belly Cheeseburger
- Spam Musubi Burgers
- Soy Garlic Chicken Wings
- Japchae Egg Rolls
- Spicy Tuna Nachos
- Tempura Cheeseburger
- Wasabi Ranch Fries
- Kimchi Grilled Cheese
- Shrimp Katsu Tacos

- Bulgogi Burrito
- Tofu Banh Mi Dogs
- Yakisoba Chili Dogs
- Furikake Popcorn Chicken
- Ssam Lettuce Burgers
- Mochiko Chicken Sandwich
- Curry Rice Fries
- Teriyaki Bacon Melt
- Korean Fried Chicken Waffles
- Uni Mac & Cheese
- Bibimbap Sliders
- Curry Ketchup Cheeseburger
- Katsu Curry Nachos
- Tonkotsu Ramen Burger
- Sweet Soy Glazed Wings
- Kalbi Cheesesteak
- Japanese Mayo Potato Salad
- Yuzu Teriyaki Meatballs
- Mentaiko Alfredo Pasta

- Spicy Gyoza Tacos
- Sweet Chili Chicken Sandwich
- Nori Fried Pickles
- Soy Egg Deviled Eggs
- Umami Burger Bombs
- Tteokbokki Poutine
- Pork Katsu Burger
- Daikon Coleslaw Dogs
- Black Garlic Cheeseburger
- Shiso Herb Fries
- Honey Butter Ramen
- Curry Udon Poppers
- Tsukune Skillet Burgers
- Seaweed BBQ Sliders

Bulgogi Cheeseburger

Ingredients:

- 1 lb ground beef
- 1/2 lb thinly sliced bulgogi beef (marinated)
- 4 brioche buns
- 4 slices cheddar cheese
- 1/2 cup kimchi, chopped
- 1 tbsp gochujang mayo (mix mayo + gochujang)
- Lettuce, tomato (optional)
- Salt & pepper to taste

Instructions:

1. Grill burger patties, seasoning with salt and pepper.
2. Sauté marinated bulgogi beef until caramelized.
3. Toast buns, then layer with burger patty, slice of cheese, bulgogi, kimchi, and gochujang mayo.
4. Serve hot with fries or pickled radish.

Kimchi Quesadilla

Ingredients:

- 2 flour tortillas
- 1/2 cup kimchi, chopped
- 1 cup shredded mozzarella or cheddar
- 1 tbsp sesame oil
- Optional: scallions, cooked chicken or tofu

Instructions:

1. Heat sesame oil in pan, lightly sauté kimchi.
2. Place one tortilla in the pan, layer with cheese, kimchi, optional protein, and more cheese.
3. Top with second tortilla, cook until golden brown on both sides.
4. Slice and serve with sour cream or spicy mayo.

Teriyaki Mac and Cheese

Ingredients:

- 2 cups elbow macaroni
- 2 tbsp butter
- 2 tbsp flour
- 2 cups milk
- 1 1/2 cups shredded cheese (cheddar/mozzarella mix)
- 1/4 cup teriyaki sauce
- Optional: scallions or sesame seeds

Instructions:

1. Cook pasta, drain, and set aside.
2. In a saucepan, melt butter, whisk in flour, cook 1 min.
3. Add milk gradually, stirring until thickened.
4. Stir in cheese until melted, then add teriyaki sauce.
5. Mix with pasta and top with scallions or sesame seeds.

Gochujang Chicken Tacos

Ingredients:

- 1 lb chicken breast or thigh, diced
- 2 tbsp gochujang
- 1 tbsp soy sauce
- 1 tsp honey
- 1 tbsp oil
- Corn or flour tortillas
- Slaw mix or shredded cabbage
- Lime wedges

Instructions:

1. Marinate chicken in gochujang, soy sauce, honey.
2. Sauté or grill until fully cooked and slightly charred.
3. Warm tortillas, fill with chicken, slaw, and a squeeze of lime.
4. Optional: drizzle with gochujang mayo.

Korean Corn Dog Bites

Ingredients:

- 4 hot dogs, cut into thirds
- 1 cup pancake mix
- 1/2 cup panko breadcrumbs
- 1 egg
- 1/3 cup milk
- Skewers or toothpicks
- Oil for frying
- Sugar (optional)

Instructions:

1. Mix pancake batter with egg and milk.
2. Skewer hot dog bites, dip in batter, roll in panko.
3. Fry until golden brown. Sprinkle lightly with sugar for Korean flair.
4. Serve with ketchup and mustard.

Miso Butter Ramen

Ingredients:

- 2 packs instant ramen (no seasoning)
- 2 tbsp white miso
- 2 tbsp butter
- 2 cloves garlic, minced
- 1/2 cup corn
- 2 boiled eggs
- Scallions and sesame seeds

Instructions:

1. Cook noodles, reserve 1/2 cup water.
2. In a pan, melt butter, add garlic and miso, stir to combine.
3. Add noodle water to thin the sauce, then toss in noodles.
4. Serve topped with corn, egg, scallions, and sesame seeds.

Sesame Sriracha Sliders

Ingredients:

- 1 lb ground beef or chicken
- 1 tbsp sesame oil
- Salt & pepper
- 2 tbsp sriracha mayo
- Slider buns
- Pickles or cucumber slices

Instructions:

1. Season and form small patties, cook until browned.
2. Toast slider buns, then layer with patty, sriracha mayo, and pickles.
3. Drizzle with extra sesame oil for flavor.

Scallion Pancake Wraps

Ingredients:

- 1 pack scallion pancakes (frozen or fresh)
- 1/2 cup cooked meat (bulgogi, pork, or tofu)
- 1/4 cup kimchi
- Lettuce or spinach

Instructions:

1. Cook scallion pancakes until crispy.
2. Layer meat, kimchi, and greens on each pancake.
3. Roll or fold like a taco or burrito and serve warm.

Pork Belly Cheeseburger

Ingredients:

- 4 pork belly slices
- 1 lb ground beef (for patties)
- 4 slices cheese (American or Swiss)
- Brioche buns
- Gochujang mayo
- Lettuce and onions

Instructions:

1. Grill or pan-sear pork belly until crispy.
2. Cook burger patties, top with cheese to melt.
3. Assemble with buns, pork belly, gochujang mayo, and toppings.

Spam Musubi Burgers

Ingredients:

- 1 can Spam, sliced
- 4 burger buns or rice buns (optional)
- Teriyaki glaze
- Fried egg (optional)
- Lettuce
- Furikake

Instructions:

1. Fry Spam slices, glaze with teriyaki sauce.
2. Toast buns or form rice buns with furikake seasoning.
3. Assemble burger with Spam, fried egg, and lettuce.
4. Serve with pickles or seaweed chips.

Soy Garlic Chicken Wings

Ingredients:

- 2 lbs chicken wings
- 1/4 cup soy sauce
- 2 tbsp honey
- 1 tbsp brown sugar
- 4 cloves garlic, minced
- 1 tsp sesame oil
- Green onions & sesame seeds (for garnish)
- Oil for frying

Instructions:

1. Fry wings until golden and crispy.
2. In a saucepan, simmer soy sauce, honey, brown sugar, garlic, and sesame oil until thickened.
3. Toss wings in sauce and garnish with green onions and sesame seeds.

Japchae Egg Rolls

Ingredients:

- 1 cup cooked japchae (Korean glass noodles)
- 6–8 egg roll wrappers
- 1 tbsp oil (for brushing or frying)
- Dipping sauce: soy sauce + rice vinegar

Instructions:

1. Place japchae in the center of each wrapper and roll tightly.
2. Fry until golden or bake at 400°F until crispy, brushing lightly with oil.
3. Serve with dipping sauce.

Spicy Tuna Nachos

Ingredients:

- 1/2 lb sushi-grade tuna, diced
- 1 tbsp mayo
- 1 tsp sriracha
- Tortilla chips or crispy wonton chips
- Avocado, diced
- Scallions & sesame seeds

Instructions:

1. Mix tuna, mayo, and sriracha.
2. Top chips with spicy tuna, avocado, scallions, and sesame seeds.
3. Serve chilled for a fresh crunch.

Tempura Cheeseburger

Ingredients:

- 1 lb ground beef
- 4 slices cheese
- 4 brioche buns
- Tempura batter (flour, egg, ice water)
- Lettuce, tomato
- Oil for frying

Instructions:

1. Cook burger patties and add cheese on top. Let cool slightly.
2. Dip each in tempura batter and deep-fry briefly until crispy.
3. Assemble with buns, lettuce, and tomato. Crunchy outside, juicy inside.

Wasabi Ranch Fries

Ingredients:

- 4 cups French fries (frozen or hand-cut)
- 1/2 cup ranch dressing
- 1 tsp wasabi paste (or to taste)
- Green onions or nori strips for topping

Instructions:

1. Cook fries until golden and crisp.
2. Mix wasabi with ranch dressing.
3. Drizzle over fries and top with green onions or crushed seaweed.

Kimchi Grilled Cheese

Ingredients:

- 2 slices thick bread
- 1/4 cup chopped kimchi
- 2 slices cheese (cheddar or mozzarella)
- Butter for grilling

Instructions:

1. Butter bread, layer cheese and kimchi inside.
2. Grill on a skillet until golden and melty.
3. Slice and enjoy the spicy, tangy crunch.

Shrimp Katsu Tacos

Ingredients:

- 1/2 lb shrimp, peeled
- Panko breadcrumbs
- Flour, egg (for dredging)
- Tortillas
- Slaw or lettuce
- Katsu sauce

Instructions:

1. Dredge shrimp in flour, egg, then panko. Fry until golden.
2. Warm tortillas, layer slaw and crispy shrimp.
3. Drizzle with katsu sauce and serve.

Bulgogi Burrito

Ingredients:

- 1/2 lb bulgogi beef
- Rice (white or fried)
- Kimchi or slaw
- Gochujang mayo
- Large flour tortillas

Instructions:

1. Cook bulgogi until caramelized.
2. Layer beef, rice, kimchi, and sauce in tortilla.
3. Wrap tightly and grill for extra crunch.

Tofu Banh Mi Dogs

Ingredients:

- Firm tofu, sliced and pan-seared
- Hot dog buns
- Pickled carrots and daikon
- Cilantro, cucumber
- Sriracha mayo

Instructions:

1. Sear tofu until golden.
2. Place in bun and top with pickled veggies, cucumber, cilantro, and spicy mayo.
3. A fun, fusion twist on the classic banh mi.

Yakisoba Chili Dogs

Ingredients:

- Yakisoba noodles, cooked and sauced
- Hot dogs
- Hot dog buns
- Optional: pickled ginger, scallions, bonito flakes

Instructions:

1. Cook hot dogs and warm buns.
2. Top with a pile of savory yakisoba noodles.
3. Garnish with ginger, scallions, or bonito flakes for a Japanese street food feel.

Furikake Popcorn Chicken

Ingredients:

- 1 lb boneless chicken thighs, cut into bite-sized pieces
- 1/2 cup cornstarch
- 2 eggs, beaten
- Salt & pepper
- Oil for frying
- Furikake seasoning

Instructions:

1. Season chicken with salt and pepper.
2. Dip in egg, then coat with cornstarch.
3. Fry until golden and crispy.
4. Sprinkle generously with furikake before serving.

Ssam Lettuce Burgers

Ingredients:

- 1 lb ground beef or pork
- 2 tbsp gochujang
- Butter or bibb lettuce leaves
- Sliced cucumber and pickled radish
- Garlic mayo or ssamjang (optional)

Instructions:

1. Form seasoned patties and grill.
2. Use lettuce leaves as the "bun" and stack with patty, veggies, and sauce.
3. Wrap and enjoy as a handheld Korean lettuce wrap burger.

Furikake Popcorn Chicken

Ingredients:

- 1 lb boneless chicken thighs, cut into bite-sized pieces
- 1/2 cup cornstarch
- 2 eggs, beaten
- Salt & pepper
- Oil for frying
- Furikake seasoning

Instructions:

1. Season chicken with salt and pepper.
2. Dip in egg, then coat with cornstarch.
3. Fry until golden and crispy.
4. Sprinkle generously with furikake before serving.

Ssam Lettuce Burgers

Ingredients:

- 1 lb ground beef or pork
- 2 tbsp gochujang
- Butter or bibb lettuce leaves
- Sliced cucumber and pickled radish
- Garlic mayo or ssamjang (optional)

Instructions:

1. Form seasoned patties and grill.
2. Use lettuce leaves as the "bun" and stack with patty, veggies, and sauce.
3. Wrap and enjoy as a handheld Korean lettuce wrap burger.

Mochiko Chicken Sandwich

Ingredients:

- 1 lb chicken thighs
- 1/2 cup mochiko flour
- 1/4 cup cornstarch
- 1 egg
- 2 tbsp soy sauce
- 1 tbsp sugar
- Brioche buns
- Slaw or lettuce
- Spicy mayo

Instructions:

1. Marinate chicken with soy sauce and sugar.
2. Dredge in mochiko and cornstarch mixture, then fry.
3. Assemble with bun, slaw, and spicy mayo.

Curry Rice Fries

Ingredients:

- 4 cups French fries
- 1/2 cup Japanese curry sauce (thickened)
- 1/4 cup cooked rice
- Scallions for garnish

Instructions:

1. Fry or bake fries until crispy.
2. Top with a scoop of rice and hot Japanese curry sauce.
3. Garnish with scallions and optional cheese.

Teriyaki Bacon Melt

Ingredients:

- 4 slices bacon
- 1/2 lb ground beef
- 4 slices cheese
- 4 slices sandwich bread or buns
- 2 tbsp teriyaki sauce
- Butter for grilling

Instructions:

1. Cook bacon and burgers, brushing patties with teriyaki sauce.
2. Stack burger, cheese, and bacon on bread.
3. Grill until golden and melty.

Korean Fried Chicken Waffles

Ingredients:

- Fried Korean chicken (drumsticks or tenders)
- Waffles (buttermilk or sweet corn)
- Honey butter or gochujang syrup
- Scallions or sesame seeds

Instructions:

1. Prepare crispy fried Korean-style chicken.
2. Stack on top of waffles.
3. Drizzle with spicy syrup or sweet butter. Serve hot.

Uni Mac & Cheese

Ingredients:

- 2 cups cooked pasta
- 1/2 cup heavy cream
- 1/2 cup shredded cheese (cheddar/parmesan)
- 1–2 tbsp uni (sea urchin), mashed
- Chopped chives (optional)

Instructions:

1. Heat cream and cheese until smooth.
2. Stir in mashed uni gently.
3. Add cooked pasta and toss.
4. Top with chives or seaweed flakes.

Bibimbap Sliders

Ingredients:

- Slider buns
- 1/2 lb ground beef or bulgogi
- Fried quail or mini eggs
- Pickled veggies (carrot, radish)
- Gochujang mayo

Instructions:

1. Cook patties or bulgogi.
2. Toast buns, spread gochujang mayo.
3. Layer patty, pickled veggies, and a small fried egg.

Curry Ketchup Cheeseburger

Ingredients:

- 1 lb ground beef
- 4 slices cheese
- 4 burger buns
- 2 tbsp curry ketchup (mix ketchup + curry powder)
- Lettuce, tomato

Instructions:

1. Cook patties, melt cheese on top.
2. Spread curry ketchup on buns.
3. Assemble burgers with fresh toppings.

Katsu Curry Nachos

Ingredients:

- Breaded pork or chicken katsu, sliced
- Tortilla or wonton chips
- Japanese curry sauce
- Mozzarella or cheddar cheese
- Scallions & pickled ginger

Instructions:

1. Bake chips topped with cheese and sliced katsu.
2. Drizzle with hot curry sauce.
3. Garnish with scallions and ginger.

Tonkotsu Ramen Burger

Ingredients:

- Ramen noodle buns (cooked, shaped, and pan-fried)
- Pork belly slices or patty
- Tonkotsu sauce or broth (reduced)
- Soft-boiled egg halves
- Green onions

Instructions:

1. Form cooked ramen into bun shapes, chill, then pan-fry until crisp.
2. Grill pork belly or burger patty.
3. Stack with tonkotsu sauce, egg, and greens between ramen buns.

Sweet Soy Glazed Wings

Ingredients:

- 2 lbs chicken wings
- 1/4 cup soy sauce
- 2 tbsp brown sugar
- 1 tbsp honey
- 1 tsp rice vinegar
- 1 tsp grated ginger
- 2 cloves garlic, minced
- Sesame seeds & scallions for garnish

Instructions:

1. Bake or fry wings until crispy.
2. Simmer soy, sugar, honey, vinegar, garlic, and ginger until thickened.
3. Toss wings in glaze and top with sesame seeds and scallions.

Kalbi Cheesesteak

Ingredients:

- 1 lb thinly sliced beef short ribs (kalbi)
- 1/2 onion, sliced
- 1 bell pepper, sliced
- Provolone or mozzarella cheese
- Hoagie rolls
- Gochujang mayo

Instructions:

1. Marinate beef in kalbi sauce, then grill or sauté.
2. Sauté onions and peppers.
3. Layer beef, veggies, and cheese in rolls. Toast until melty. Add spicy mayo.

Japanese Mayo Potato Salad

Ingredients:

- 2 cups boiled, cubed potatoes
- 1/4 cup Japanese mayo (Kewpie)
- 1 tsp rice vinegar
- 1/4 cup cucumber, thinly sliced
- 1 boiled egg, chopped
- Salt, pepper, and optional corn

Instructions:

1. Mix all ingredients until creamy.
2. Chill and serve with extra Kewpie drizzle on top.

Yuzu Teriyaki Meatballs

Ingredients:

- 1 lb ground chicken or turkey
- 2 tbsp breadcrumbs
- 1 egg
- 2 tbsp yuzu juice
- 1/4 cup teriyaki sauce
- Scallions & sesame seeds

Instructions:

1. Mix meat, egg, breadcrumbs, and seasonings. Form into meatballs.
2. Bake or pan-fry until cooked.
3. Simmer in teriyaki + yuzu until glazed.

Mentaiko Alfredo Pasta

Ingredients:

- 8 oz pasta
- 2 tbsp butter
- 1/2 cup heavy cream
- 1–2 tbsp mentaiko (pollock roe), removed from sac
- 1 clove garlic, minced
- Parmesan, nori strips, or green onion for topping

Instructions:

1. Cook pasta.
2. In a pan, melt butter, add garlic, cream, and mentaiko. Stir until smooth.
3. Toss with pasta and top with parmesan or nori.

Spicy Gyoza Tacos

Ingredients:

- Gyoza filling (ground pork, garlic, ginger, cabbage)
- Small tortillas or wonton taco shells
- Spicy dipping sauce (soy, vinegar, chili oil)
- Green onions

Instructions:

1. Cook gyoza filling and season well.
2. Fill tacos with hot filling and drizzle with spicy sauce.
3. Garnish with scallions or sesame seeds.

Sweet Chili Chicken Sandwich

Ingredients:

- Fried chicken breast or thigh
- 2 tbsp sweet chili sauce
- Brioche bun
- Lettuce or slaw
- Mayo or cream cheese spread

Instructions:

1. Fry or bake chicken until crispy.
2. Toss in or drizzle with sweet chili sauce.
3. Stack in bun with slaw and creamy spread.

Nori Fried Pickles

Ingredients:

- Dill pickle slices
- Nori sheets, shredded or powdered
- Batter (flour, egg, panko or tempura)
- Oil for frying

Instructions:

1. Dredge pickles in batter, coat with crushed nori.
2. Fry until golden and serve with wasabi ranch or spicy mayo.

Soy Egg Deviled Eggs

Ingredients:

- 6 soy sauce marinated eggs (cut in half)
- 1 tbsp Kewpie mayo
- 1 tsp wasabi or mustard
- Dash of soy sauce
- Nori or furikake to garnish

Instructions:

1. Scoop yolks, mix with mayo, wasabi, and soy sauce.
2. Pipe back into whites and top with garnish.

Umami Burger Bombs

Ingredients:

- 1 lb ground beef or umami-seasoned mushroom mix
- 1 tbsp soy sauce
- 1 tsp miso paste
- Cheese cubes (cheddar or mozzarella)
- Slider buns or bao buns

Instructions:

1. Mix beef with soy and miso.
2. Form around cheese cubes into mini balls.
3. Bake or grill until cooked and gooey inside. Serve in buns.

Tteokbokki Poutine

Ingredients:

- Korean rice cakes (tteok), boiled
- 1 cup fries (shoestring or crinkle)
- 1/2 cup tteokbokki sauce (gochujang, soy, sugar, garlic)
- 1/4 cup shredded mozzarella or cheese curds
- Scallions & sesame seeds

Instructions:

1. Bake or fry the fries.
2. Sauté rice cakes in sauce until coated and tender.
3. Layer fries, tteokbokki, cheese, and garnish. Broil until melty if desired.

Pork Katsu Burger

Ingredients:

- 2 pork cutlets, breaded and fried
- Shredded cabbage
- Tonkatsu sauce
- Brioche or milk buns

Instructions:

1. Fry pork cutlets until crispy.
2. Toast buns and layer with pork, cabbage, and tonkatsu sauce.
3. Serve with pickles or wasabi mayo on the side.

Daikon Coleslaw Dogs

Ingredients:

- Hot dog buns and grilled sausages
- Daikon slaw (julienned daikon, carrot, vinegar, sesame oil)
- Japanese mayo
- Toasted sesame seeds

Instructions:

1. Make quick daikon slaw and chill.
2. Grill sausages and place in buns.
3. Top with slaw, mayo, and sesame seeds.

Black Garlic Cheeseburger

Ingredients:

- 1 lb ground beef
- Black garlic cloves (mashed)
- Cheese (aged cheddar or gouda)
- Burger buns
- Arugula or caramelized onions

Instructions:

1. Mix black garlic paste into patties. Grill to preference.
2. Top with cheese, greens or onions, and serve on toasted buns.

Shiso Herb Fries

Ingredients:

- 2 cups fries
- 1 tbsp shiso leaves, finely chopped
- Salt
- Optional: furikake or lemon zest

Instructions:

1. Cook fries until golden.
2. Toss with chopped shiso, salt, and optional toppings.
3. Serve with yuzu mayo or spicy ketchup.

Honey Butter Ramen

Ingredients:

- 1 pack instant ramen, drained
- 1 tbsp butter
- 1 tbsp honey
- Pinch of garlic powder
- Green onions and sesame seeds

Instructions:

1. Cook and drain ramen.
2. Toss with melted butter, honey, and seasoning.
3. Garnish and serve hot for a sweet-savory treat.

Curry Udon Poppers

Ingredients:

- 1 cup thick udon noodles, chopped
- 1/4 cup Japanese curry sauce (thick)
- 2 tbsp cheese
- 1 egg
- Panko for coating
- Oil for frying

Instructions:

1. Mix noodles, curry, cheese, and egg into a sticky mixture.
2. Shape into balls, coat in panko.
3. Deep fry until crispy and golden.

Tsukune Skillet Burgers

Ingredients:

- 1 lb ground chicken
- 2 tbsp soy sauce
- 1 tbsp mirin
- 1 tsp grated ginger
- Egg yolk (for dipping)
- Burger buns or rice buns

Instructions:

1. Form chicken mixture into thick patties.
2. Pan-sear in a skillet with a glaze of soy/mirin/sugar.
3. Serve in buns or over rice with an egg yolk dip.

Seaweed BBQ Sliders

Ingredients:

- Mini burger buns
- BBQ beef or pulled pork
- Roasted seaweed sheets or flakes
- Pickled daikon or onions
- Gochujang BBQ sauce

Instructions:

1. Warm BBQ meat and mix with gochujang BBQ sauce.
2. Stack in slider buns with seaweed and pickled veggies.
3. Serve as a small-plate or appetizer dish.

www.ingramcontent.com/pod-product-compliance
Lightning Source LLC
LaVergne TN
LVHW081324060526
838201LV00055B/2443

9798349302466